Candied Honey

Pam Cole

Candied Honey

Candied Honey
ISBN 978 1 76041 549 5
Copyright © text Pam Cole 2018
Cover: *New England Sunrise*, Col Levy

First published 2018 by
Ginninderra Press
PO Box 3461 Port Adelaide 5015
www.ginninderrapress.com.au

Contents

Author's note	9
Candied Honey	11
At Eighty-one	12
Swinging	13
January	14
The Question	15
February	16
At Dusk, 1940s	17
Belladonna Lilies	18
Harvesting	19
March, Ending	20
The Student	21
A Reply For Dale	22
A Word of Thanks to Judith Wright	23
Scribbly-gum	24
Cherry Tree in Late Autumn	25
Parrots and Olive Trees	26
Old Fence Posts	27
Dark Matter	28
Christmas at Home	29
Skin	30
Foxes	31
The Steers	32
Grandma's Hats, 1999	33
Sideshow Alley, 1944	34
Midnight Window	35
December Evening	36
Driving to Tumut	37
Generations	38
A Sort-of Haiku	39

Spaces	40
Going On	41
Christmas Day 2015	42
Finding Old Tools	43
At a Harbourside Restaurant	44
Hard Comfort	46
Tears on Snow	47
Doves	48
Plums	49
Black Cockatoos	50
Heat and Hay Mulch	51
Dragonfly	52
Magpies	53
Wrens	54
Late August	55
At Maleny	56
The Orchard	57
To a Nine-year-old	58
An Old Letter, Read in Autumn	59
Gloria Yates	60
London Foxes	61
Haymaking	62
The Butterfly	63
Jonquils	64
Stars	65
The Aunts	66
Kin	67
The Nightingale	68
Honeyeaters	69
Agapanthus	70
The Outback	71
At Bonny Hills	72

Norfolk Island Pine	73
Grandmother Lily's Babies	74
November Dawn	75
Child and Bushfire, 1942	76
Last Day of Winter	77
Saying Goodbye	78
Green Sky	79
Visiting the Specialists	80
Plover	81
Beethoven's Child	82
Two Weddings…Tuncurry and Kosovo	83
Breath Music	84
Courage	85
Near Black Bob's Creek, Southern Highlands, NSW	86
Rainbow Bee-eaters	88
Song Strata	90
Peeling Peaches	91
Driving North	93
Pelican	95
After Winter Rain	96
Jacaranda	97
King Parrots	98
Not the TV News	99
Epitaph for a Very Small Dog	100
Bad Weather	101
Two Roses	102
Autumn Afternoon	104

Author's note

At first I intended the title of this book to be *Scribbly-gum*, but as my eighty-second birthday crept up on me during a glorious autumn and we made preparations for winter – storing firewood, stocking the pantry, clearing garden debris – I recalled long-ago winters, with the old kitchen clock and the honeypot kept warm on the brick surround of the wood-burning stove, and I changed my mind.

Candied Honey

Honey in summer pours and spreads and glows,
trickles from the spoon, delights the eye
with swirls and squiggles, sticks to fingers,
makes of toast a joy.
Left on the shelf in winter, honey holds
a different secret, for it turns in crystal-slowness
to another self. The colour goes
from rosy amber to an ochre glow, a grainy gold,
and slowly thickens to its candied form.
Its somehow-buttery feel, yet gritty-firm,
tingles my fingers yet, remembering.
And prudent mothers set the jar through winter
not near the kettles or the spitting pan
but well back in the smoky-blackened recess of the stove
quite near the chimney flue for warmth, and where
the weary ticking of the tired kitchen clock
told us its stiff old cogs were grateful of such care.

At Eighty-one

My elderly muse grunts, feet splayed,
hands pressed to knees helping her rise,
rubs at her shoulder, her back, growls
an expletive aimed at bodily weakness,
at easy chairs and their short-term comfort,
at obvious statements, old jokes, lukewarm tea,
the wrong biscuits – scowls at the telly and stifles
a sob as her old bones grind together.
When did she last come bustling down
out of the orchard, her apron a hammock
for bulges of windfall pears, leaves in her hair,
dogs trailing around her through hayfields of grass,
unspoken messages trapped in her head,
eyes sparking, coming to get me,
to snap out her orders, bully me back to work?
She was grey even then, and those bounding dogs are dead.
There are others, beloved as they, and the grass
whispers again of the fires, the fatiguing sun,
makes its fierce music. Small apples roll,
the cockies screech overhead, leaves rustle,
the heat throbs its thundery beat,
and I think that I'll walk – if I walk, maybe the rhythm
will thrum from my feet to my head in its old way,
maybe the words will return.

Swinging

Curled like tadpoles, like insects,
the children cling to the swinging rope.
Over the water they fly, squealing,
arms taut, knees doubled-up,
drop with triumphant yells into the river,
snort with delight and spin sun
from their wet hair on emerging.
Someone's big brother turns kindly to me,
says, 'You lining up for a go?' and I
laughingly, one eye on the grandkids, say
that I'd love to. 'I'd bet,' says he,
from his good teenage heart, 'bet you've done this
plenty times back in the day.'
'From willows,' I said, 'not rope.'
And while I could see my reply making sense,
(rope being likely not invented way back then),
I was lost in the long-ago swish and the tangle
of willow boughs swinging wild over the water,
the rasping of wet woollen bathers, the squeals,
the rip through the leaves, the flying, the splash.

January

The days spin by.
It's like the old movies
where calendar leaves peel off,
whisking into the dark.
Here it's half-January.
Summer's still going to bake us
(in that dumbest of modern phrases)
twenty-four-seven –
it's still holding the threat of fire,
sends snakes through our grass,
a blitzkrieg of wasps,
and the drownings of children.
Yet that spin brings the wildest of winds,
a chill in the mornings,
toadstools spotting the grass,
and a general feel of unease.
I find myself longing for autumn,
but my toes curl tight on the brink.

The Question

When I asked of the moon
(as one does a child)
'And how old are you?'
it beamed like a baby
wordless and bland,
didn't know, didn't care,
sailed in eternal silence.
Left me, a fool, on the dry
spangled grass, quite alone.

February

Bugs have made lace of the cherry leaves.
Limp-wristed lily stems droop on the verge.
The bold faced moon's just an observer.
Smoke lies wearily over the hills.
Rose petals crumple like tissue, turn brown.
She's tired, old summer, even though
the melons have sweetened, the plums
hang glowing with juice under the boughs,
the skinks and the blue-tongue flick over the stones;
she's had quite enough of the school playground clamour
of cockatoos ripping the orchard apart and the effort
of pinning a smile to her face. She'll be glad
when the mornings rise over the hills
a little bit north of the valley, the shadows
less sharply incised on the grass,
when autumn takes over her shift.

At Dusk, 1940s

'Oh well…the fall of Singapore…'
Kids' ears catch things you'd never know.
'Just got out in time. Last ones, to hear her talk…'
Cut crystal crackles in her words, masks her apprehension.
Tea on the veranda, friends under flickering
shadows of the vine, wisteria lilac-pink upon grey lattice.
Not knowing how our mother's words belong, I watch the
　pretty lady
pass us and repass – dark pompadour and pageboy,
skirt flipping round her knees, sandals
that at seven I could die for, laced and crisscrossed
round her ankles like a ballet girl, bolero with chic puff sleeves
'*Ong-ray, ong-ray*, she's saying,' smirks a giggler…
another sips, and murmurs, 'We did hear she's French…'
Passing and repassing, stroller pushed before her,
baby snoozing undisturbed as dusk comes down,
and passing and repassing, endlessly she calls,
'Honoré, Honoré!'
　　　　　My mother ends
the conversation with a brisk 'Her little boy…no, no,
too late, they couldn't get him out in time,'
glances meaningly in our direction, pours the tea.
She haunts my memory for ever after,
with stroller wheels arattle, smiling, hopeful,
passing and repassing in the dusk.

Belladonna Lilies

Pearlier than baby's skin,
throat lit with green, stilt-legged,
like flamingos wading.

Harvesting

'War against Terror'
our gallant leaders claim –
and all I can think is how
my roses burn with beauty,
hay smells sweet,
and moonlight's like white magic,
and that the books all say
before 'The War to End all Wars'
the harvest was prolific
and the roses would amaze.

March, Ending

Wasps tangle in the silk tree,
dip to gather water,
zot and bumble into corners
underneath the shade cloth,
dithering over building sites.
I sit wet and stinging
from the chill blue of what's set
to be the last swim of this summer;
there's a twiggy case moth glued
for its brief forever underneath the roof,
the decking has forgotten scorching sun
but hums and creaks a little underfoot,
warmed and flaking.
Thunder rolls and cracks the sky –
the dog's decided wisdom is the better part,
scooted up indoors and left me
scraping sneakers onto slickened skin,
and wondering if summer's really gone.

The Student

'Viruses,' she said,
'they've found viruses
are really minute spaceships –
messaging by antennae,
putting down landing-legs,
anchoring on with grappling feet,
making their own moon landings;
our gut colonised with bacteria
that make executive decisions:
how we'll grow, what we'll eat,
how develop…'
   'Mmm-mh!' I said,
and went on chopping the pumpkin.

A Reply For Dale

Yackandandah, 12.4.17

What she said of twilight has me stumped,
buttering her toast and staring through
my smudgy windows at our amethyst
and garnet-glowing hills, and burbling on
about the hour of day when all horizons blur
and people with them, until all
that's left is timeless gauzy colour,
shifting dreams, humanity and its persona
faded into hazy nothingness, adrift
and shifting like the light dissolving into darkness
but permeating all the world with dreamy glow.

A Word of Thanks to Judith Wright

Picking and pecking among my files
for pages to fill this book – how many,
I found, told of birds, scribbled them,
sketched them in clumsy phrases.
A remembrance came, how in my youth
your bird poems puzzled my mind
for their reason, their depth –
and how in my age birds and their ways
are significant too – and I'd grown enough,
what with life and its battles, to know
now, at last, a little of what you were saying.
Bending stiffly, and flashing a torch,
I searched on the bookshelves to find
a small jewel case spilling out
lyrebird, dotterel, black cockatoo,
parrot and pelican, each with its
faceted levels of meaning –
such treasuries of words, such
wisdom held within.
I hardly dare
to let mine see the light of day.

Scribbly-gum

Kids know magic.
We'd read the message of the scribbly-gum,
that cursive scrawling on the smooth
and satin trunk below the bark,
heeded its message,
went about our ways.
And some days, when the sky held thunder
or a rainbow dazed our eyes,
we read the music annotated there
in magic scribbles, even sang its songs.

Cherry Tree in Late Autumn

Here under the cherry tree,
smoke veiling the hills and adrift in the valley,
yellow leaves float to my feet
and my knitting hands rest.
Mahogany leaves on the roses,
sunshine as gentle as honey,
chrysanthemums bursting with colour
and rosemary, lavender, sage in echoing blue.
So the thrum of an aircraft, soft on the ear amid bird sound,
then throbbing and flailing the air
as it circles its dragonfly way,
at first brings alarm, but it's only
the fire-watch chopper doing its rounds.
And the sun burns my wrists and reminds me
of chores left unfinished,
and writing that's yet to be done.

Parrots and Olive Trees

Late on a stormy afternoon,
with pomegranates glowing on the tree,
when seven shades of gold rang out
from the persimmon leaves behind the grey
and feathery blue of emu-bush,
the dog and I walked out.
Down past the rough and storied
row of fence posts, logged and adzed
so long ago, and past the rose
and crimson vine whose leaves spill now
upon the rocks below,
and down we went, to where a row
of olive trees were giggling,
were throwing up their hands –
no, wait! It was three parrots all awhirl
and chuckling as they feasted on the fruit.

Old Fence Posts

Look how they lean,
unsure of their surroundings,
salvaged from a storm-smashed fence,
hauled out from underneath the broken boughs.
Once they were trees themselves,
sprang up as seedlings, God knows where,
some hillside where the wild birds flew.
Too old to weep, too long they've stood,
stout farmhands holding taut the wire
that's now so rusted it was broken by the fall.
Too long for tears, yet as my hand
falls gently on their roughness you can tell
some longing lingers – to return,
to be back where the long grass flows
and birdsong ripples as the roos slope by.

Dark Matter

Astrophysicists' studies…'harmony of the universe'…'way the equations hang together so felicitously'…lead to the conclusion of some creative force not yet understood

To prove it exists, to measure and map dark matter,
to number the universe, scientists drop miles deep in a miners' cage
and pacing the salt mine's corridors
fill its glittering chambers with wizardry,
preparing a trap. Neutrinos, which bombard all matter,
must sometime reveal themselves in a bar of crystal,
their image expanded into visibility by the mathematical magic
locked in a shimmering cup-like shape. This will detect the light
given off by colliding particles of matter. Their interest lies
in trapping for their study that dark secret which controls
the movement of the universe.
        But see, this documentary:
helmeted, armoured, they move slow-gauntleted to hold
with reverent touch a shimmer-fragile chalice,
join it to the crystal bar, submerging all with druid gravity.
What? Helms and gauntlets and this chalice cup, once more…
was it for this that, slow as galaxies,
old Merlin crept through time into his crystal tomb?
Does he lie here with the secrets of the universe,
counting the infinite music of the stars?

Christmas at Home

Christmas at home meant roses, grapes, earth baked to crackle-ware,
night skies theatrical and doomy with electric storms,
fruit salad with our single taste of cherries for the year.

Christmas at home meant poultry roasting in the wood-fired oven,
richly delicate gravy seething in the blackened pan.
Magic alone ruled who would find the lucky wishbone.

Christmas at home meant dodging whirly-winds of dust,
racing with squinted eyes to fetch the wood heap chips,
or snatch at whiskered Santas thistle-downing by.

Christmas at home meant nuts to shell, the cracker polished shiny for the day.
Too many walnuts gave a stinging tongue. Nineteen-forty, nineteen-fifty;
Joys were strong and simple. Christmas had a flavour then.

Skin

Peach bloom once
is now crushed velvet.
Satin-smooth,
now crêpe de Chine.
Curves that clung to the bone
swing lax, and
silken arm-skin droops
like crumpled stockings.

But kisses burn
and older skin can flame.
Outside the fireflies
drift in shower-sparks,
lightning's heat rash
splashes in the summer dark,
but no more fiery and magic than
our flash and fusion of affection and desire.

Foxes

The long-drawn evening shadows camouflage them,
two foxes hidden by the rusty grasses,
trotting in line astern, intent on the trail of water,
loping in lean lines to slake their thirst at the swamp.

The Steers

Amenable and gentle,
see their baby faces raised
to seek out what's required,
and see them amiably amble down the race.
Even newly-bought, they come to us
for hay-bale sweeties at our call.
We should be happy owning ten fine steers
to fatten – there's the rub – to truck away –
ah yes. So that's the reason why
I woke this morning from a searing dream
of children coaxed into captivity.

Grandma's Hats, 1999

After the funeral, after asparagus rolls and the fruit cake,
my cousin the hostess tugged me aside.
Bobbing down with that grunt we all give once we're fifty,
she rummaged behind the glass-fronted cabinet doors
and *Here!* she said, surfacing, sparkling with laughter over her grief
and turning to show. On her matronly curls sat a little black saucer
with follow-me-lads of ribbon aflirt at the back. *And for you* –
a navy blue straw with a pitiful once roguish rose.
Both had a band of elastic and grosgrain that clung to the head
holding the hat perched chicly askew, and a veil
of the kind women prinked with gloved hands in the thirties,
hooking it daintily up to the hat brim in church or the concert,
plucking it down as she broached the hot weather outdoors.
though such fribbles don't fit with my image of grandma –
aproned in sacking on washday, in floral for stirring the jam,
her lacing-up shoes, her tremulous hands –
when these hats were new she was younger than we were today.
What tune did she hum as she anchored that straw with a hat pin?
What hopes did she hold as she hurried pit-pat down the street?

There we stood facing each other, two sixtyish cousins,
so full of memory that moment, and all unaware
of the sharp-sparking stares and the curious murmurs
of family around us. Resuming her role as the host:
They were Granma's, she told them, *My mother had kept them
in hatboxes under her bed.* And she moved away chatting and
    soothing,
mourning her mother, tending her duty and pushing her
    childhood aside.
She left me with hats in my hands and a head full of dreams.

Sideshow Alley, 1944

Back in the days when
Fatty and Skinny were comic,
when you paid sixpence to peel back
iron-hard canvas and shuffle through sawdusted grass
in the stinking hot tent, darting shy looks
and away at the World's Fattest Woman,
'funny' eluded us.
She pinned us like moths,
malevolent eyes hard as beads in dough
over a vicious red-rosebud smile, over flesh
dimpled and ringed with weight
and exhausted-elephant legs.
Stifling our nervous gasps, backing away,
appalled by her wheeze enticing the bumpkin boys
'come round the back o' the tent…?'
Safe again in the glare and the blaring of Show Day,
but never aware enough to be sorry
till now; I still feel her fury, but it's now
when ageing has taught me so much
that pity engulfs me.

Midnight Window

Night folds in pleats,
hangings as stifling and dusty as curtains
over the cinema stage in our childhood.
Oh, the down-lights made shimmers of richness
transforming stale velvet worn thin,
but promises, promises, that was the tune.
Now night drapes heavily,
thick with frog music one moment,
the next shimmers in moonlit silence…
The next fold's striped with piping bird calls, with worry;
and after that folding and rolling with thunder.
Our bones ache with it, our heads heavy
and stiff-necked and laden with years.
Promises. Yes, but…
Promising what…?

December Evening

Agapanthus pokes
stiff fingers in blue gloves.
Gaura wafts moth petals in the air.
Abseiling caterpillars dangle from the vines.
Spent geranium heads,
umbrella spokes blown upside by the wind.
Rose climbers push
their new mahogany leafage through the old.
Nigella's lost its love-in-a-mist look,
shed petals, helmeted itself in martial green.
And down the hill
a squabble of ducks erupts,
splatters from the dam, argues its way to bed.

Driving to Tumut

Hills in khaki-drab shrug shoulders
pucker-seamed with rocks.
Poplars sketch rough charcoal strokes
along the river gullies. Hot skies,
despite the air con, burn the skin.
The car spins on, climbing the neat black road
that curves and rises, curves and rises still.

Generations

Among my grown children and their brood
I am shrunk to an elf,
cross as a gouty gnome, and as ready to spit
bad cess at the passing of Time
as any malevolent fairy.

A Sort-of Haiku

You returned my verses
pinned through with logic,
poor butterflies.

Spaces

Around Junee
spoonfuls of light
spread flat across the plain.
Wheat's up. It glows green
over paddocks near as wide as oceans.

But at Dorrigo
tidal waves of mountains
range and roll beyond
the eyes' reach. Further yet
the sea's horizon spreads below the sky.

Going On

for Col Levy

There's an Antarctica
clangs and rolls around us,
freezes blood, chills action,
weights the limbs.
Sastrugi rattle bone-like.
At our feet crevasses crack.
Sled dogs, heaving at the weight,
we battle on.

Christmas Day 2015

That was a shock;
that old face in the window.
Doesn't the camera know that it's me
glancing up at the wrong time,
here in my son's garden with a rose for the old dog's grave?
Later the wrens pinkling over the lawn,
wagtails zit-zitting among leaves,
hot gusts of eucalypt-scented air,
smoke like torn tissue over the hills,
all worked their magic.
Just being there was peace.

Finding Old Tools

Even the names of the found objects are old
(wheat-bag, sugar-bag, farrier's tools)
but so familiar they rasp the heart.
Finding them packed so hopefully away,
rusty-powdered, rolled in oily rag,
it was the trust went in their packing that undid me –
wrapped bushman-style in fine-wove sugar-bag sacking
and tied with binder twine, and thrust into the toe
of country living's carryall, the wheat-bag,
on the day he knew his farming days were over.
So familiar, too, the old procedure –
humpbacked, hunch-knee'd, cradling the hoof,
and brown arms elbowing to and fro to wield the rasp;
brown hands that flex to snap the pincers shut
(*see here's the pinchers Dad!*) and *clip* the hoof is trimmed
and blue-black, snipped, its rind falls to the dust;
and then that heart-stop hammering on the knee
that pounds the square nails through the square-holed shoe.
His hand smoothes roughly round and gives a pat,
it strokes the fetlock, slides the shod hoof down
with 'Right as rain now, mate!'
O farmer, father, farrier, can't you ironclad my heart?

At a Harbourside Restaurant

Lunching at the Starfish we no longer rushed
to peer below the wharf at things aswirl
beneath the water, gape at barnacles like boils
on mammoth legs below the jetty, peer through shreds of weed
for darting shoals or hope there'd be
a broil of fins and tentacles.
We sat down, glad to do so, being sixty. Soaked up sun,
we sipped and chatted, watched the ships go by.
The whiting was delicious, the salads fine,
the conversation quiet. Best of all,
was being there together, we the elders of our younger-cousin brood,
all parents gone and older cousins
getting near the brink. To catch an eye
that held the spark known from an uncle, hear the sharp
edge to a joke like mother's, feel the gentleness
and spirit of my father's blood, rewarded
the long travel and fatigue that brought us here. But no,
we didn't rush and scramble to the water
though the old delight was there.

Tugs and ferries creamed the water, childhood escapades
got tangled in our talk of charities, retirement,
wetland conservation, birdlife, books, and still
the child in me was dabbling fingers in the water,
slipping on the seaweed, bawling as the broken glass
beneath the water stabbed my foot,
and uncles aunts and parents sighed what-did-I-say,
and this-is-what-you-get-for-skipping-Sunday-school…
we were soaking up the sun of simply living, well aware
of Time's old convolutions and the new idea
just forming, that perhaps we're 'getting on'.
For we were lunching at the Starfish
and were ten-year-olds no more.

Hard Comfort

for a dear friend mourning her mother

Sit here and take comfort.
Don't keep saying 'I know it, I know it, can't help it,'
and turning your face away like a young boy surfing,
shaking and flicking your head to rid it of tears –
will you not listen and hold to the riches I offer:
we are all dying, all grow old in our time, as she
is tearing your heart out by doing, as we
will do to our children. The comfort I offer,
the hardest comfort of all, is the knowing
and to build upon it if you can.

Tears on Snow

Thinking of the ancient legend
where children's tears produced from snow
the bamboo shoots to feed their ailing mother,
I am stabbed with tender sharpness
as their emerging green jabs soil.
I will not weep, but for my mother's memory
plant snowdrops on my lawn.

Doves

Blue air floats above the valley.
Eagle wings scribe spirals in the sky.
Lilies smoulder smoky-blue beneath the pines,
heat hums, when plain as a sip of tea,
soothing as fingertips,
such a commonplace peace is brought
by the stroll of the four o'clock doves.
Soft and as gentle as breath – as customary –
their sensible afternoon walk moves velvety over the grass,
pauses to dip heads, consider the seeds,
agreeably ambles, moves by, is silently gone from the path,
leaving a whisper of peace.

Plums

Plums echo the thundercloud's colour,
hang just as heavily low,
soften the air with their ripening scent.
Their names tumbled roughly in old Ana's voice,
Sugarplum, dis one…maybe is President…
then…don't know in English…but…
coming next D'Agen…oh, dis Angelina…
Where now are Ana and Branko
who planted these trees; who came to Australia
lugging a suitcase, wearing their name tags,
with only each other for something familiar?
Where – in this world or the next?
Reaching for fruit in the orchard they made,
planning my pickles and jam, I remember their shelves
that glowed with her jars, with his wine, remember
their weary old backs, and give thanks,
hoping they know that we care.

Black Cockatoos

Creaking like deckchairs,
black cockies flap overhead.
Presaging rain? Well, the news
and the weather girl tell us it's 40 again for this week.
Smoke over the hills.
The paddocks are crackling with heat.
Fire at Leneva, midway between us and town;
mozzie-like choppers are hovering,
swoop overhead to the dam and return.
Black leaves like cockatoo feathers
drop on our yellowing lawn.

Heat and Hay Mulch

Uphill from the shed, boots sliding on concrete.
The barrow catches on the edge; tell myself I can do it.
A biscuit of hay slides from the bale, *whoomp* in a puff of straw,
and the heat and the slope almost defeat me.
One more, just one, though something in the rib cage thumps;
Think how the garden feels: soil almost whistles with the heat,
leaves curl and dwindle, sprigs contort…there's no escape
till soft and wispy hay folds down and shades the soil.
One more. Concrete, gravel, grass, move slow beneath my feet,
transport me to the haystack. One more, blade slices twine,
the bale slides down and hay dust chokes the air.
It seems it should ignite, so powerful the heat.

Dragonfly

All morning, tracking down the buzz,
that desperate *help me*;
swiped sticky webs, shook curtains,
rattled blinds, poked corners.
At noon the blinds, slit open in the heat,
revealed the pleader.
Oh gently in the scooped palm,
Oh quickly so the fragile wings don't break –
and out, to hang a moment in blue air
unmoving, thankful, stunned,
and then away.

Magpies

Hard beak and harder eye don't fool me.
We're parents, both.
You stand silent, asking, on the lawn.
Background noise: insistent, yawping,
gimme-gimme from your young.
'Good bird,' I say, 'good bird,' and toss
the morning's crust.
Your partner drops, enquires, keeps distant.
You come hobble-hop,
hobble-hop on crisping grass
knowing my voice, trusting – almost – that food
comes with that sound.
It's sorely needed: three!
One snatching, gargling hobbledehoy –
one needing food poked beak to beak –
and one your mate flies off to, gob full of crusts
straight to the nest.
'Good bird, good bird,' I say.
You give to me brief company, carillons of song –
and joy, remembering that long ago
I too fed my young.

Wrens

The day tossed me a tumble of wrens –
no sound – silent flickers of movement,
mouse-hopping on their toothpick legs.
Hushed and mushroom-brown, wee jennies
tittup and prink along the path; in single file, up-tails
almost the height of mown grass, not quite;
curtsey to inspect a seed, bib-bob away;
so welcome – minute, delicate, a fragile gift.

Late August

Summer's on the horizon,
muttering, rolling over in bed,
reaching out for her sunnies,
rummaging into the wardrobe
for last year's thongs.
Humming like hot-weather bees,
thumping around like thunder
she scatters the morning dew;
wilfully puffing a fag end
of bushfire smoke,
ready for anything, rough as bags,
ending our softness, *bringing it on*.

At Maleny

for Doug Eaton, luthier

In the luthier's workshop music dangles in the air,
lies sleeping in the stacked wood, sings silent in the planed curve.
Unborn scraps and shards of music twirl on wires.
From the beams the notes hang mute –
a strip, a chip of this, parabola of that,
an arabesque as yet unformed and far from shaping sound,
hold their breath, await the gentle hand.
Till timber's cured or tinted, coaxed to shape,
their incense-perfumed sawdust piles and floats.
Blackwood, cedar, rosewood, scent the air.
Curve-bellied lute, sweet dulcimer, they sleep,
not yet becoming song.

The Orchard

The trees wear businesslike
straight skirts and slender sleeves
brisk, workaday,
in plain no-nonsense bark.

Last month their golden cloaks
shone swirling in the wind.
(in summer, preggie smocks and cradled
plump-fruit progeny

and leading up to that,
the frothy bridal flounce
and frill of crinoline).
Ah yes – and soon

with knobbled knees
and limbs akink with rheumatiz
they'll stand in black
enduring winter's chills.

To a Nine-year-old

Just before you go
Stop here a while.
Stay nine.
For ten so soon becomes thirteen
and then you're gone.
It's different in your teens
and little boys who'd lovingly confide
(though every bit as dear)
become articulate
in languages that adults cannot hear.
Stay close a moment more.
Let's stand here by the apple tree
and feel the sun.

An Old Letter, Read in Autumn

'Is not old wine wholesomest, old pippins toothsomest
…and old loves soundest?' – Charles Kingsley

Cotoneaster's flush
With brightened berries,
smoke-bush branches
pen-strokes of scarlet
through the cold.
Burn-off smoke airbrushes silver
against blue.

That rush of flame
you wrote of,
trees in autumn Armidale,
has echoes here,
memories in ambush, and,
Old loves – I thought –
Old pippins and old wine.
They bring a rush
of sweetness to the heart.

Gloria Yates

Autumn in Victoria.
Frost burn-off hazing hills
like Chinese silk in shades of misty blue.
Rusty leaves, and here and there
a star of crusty-gold chrysanthemum,
sparks in the veiled light.
The dogs lay dozing.
Fleece slipped through my fingers
as the wheel whirred.
Peaceful.
The dogs of all the world loved Glor,
and mine with one accord
raised muzzles, howled,
and slept again. No doubt they knew.

London Foxes

Mum, she said, *y'know when I called*
last month that there were baby foxes?
We saw fox cubs from our high window?
So sweet, so tiny by the garden wall?
They've grown, they jump across,
go hunting – guess what Mum:
they bring home treasures, potsherds,
feathers, scraps of plastic…
I could see them, thought of how for me
walled-in by illness, hemmed by distance
and the tangled overgrowth of life's accretions,
she'd piled in phone calls all her scraps of treasure,
bits of her to smooth her absence,
made me see a flick of ragged fur,
of pipe-stem muzzles, skinny feet ascramble –
not just foxes, she was sending glimpses
of her patchwork London day.

Haymaking

Came news an old friend died.
Age, the implacable foe, had mown her down
and we left standing, grasses
that still can bend – white-haired, booted,
and sweating – tossing our new-mown hay,
as a storm builds over the afternoon.
We are raking the hay on the flat
peasant style, slowed by our old joints
but swinging in unison, garnering bundles to fling
filling the trailer, one eye on the weather
and one on the hay fork's swing,
while the cattle nose round, lipping the straw,
gleaning the scraps for sweetness.

The Butterfly

A scrap of wrinkled silk,
a twist of orange ribbon
tangled in dry grass?
I bent to look…
it was one wing, unfolding,
while the other, rolled
and furled like an umbrella,
tugged its tip from out the casing,
uncrinkling slowly in the sun.

A message waited
when I'd wandered home:
She's gone.
Guess that was you Ruth,
slipping the old crushed chrysalis
and opening your wings
to new and glorious flight.

Jonquils

It's
all very well for jonquils
parading in rows, blowing their own trumpets,
their gold blare and lemon fanfare welcoming winter;
but I'm cold as an old tree and my limbs creak,
any flowers I wore are fallen,
and I see the end of the road
near.

Stars

Pink stars on green pasture;
I know it's onion weed,
but I'm that cantankerous creature, a poet,
so for me it's joyous confetti,
a floral carpet, pink stars
in an upside-down sky of spring green.

The Aunts

Death of the second-last aunt, and a fortnight ago we had two –
both silvery, fragile, faded and crumpled but smiling –
and before that a bounty, a bouquet, a blessing of aunts.
Till they took it into their heads (this notion of dwindling),
the lot of them phoned one another and visited, sent funny
    cards,
wrote haystacks of letters, *kept up* with it all.

Those monoliths of our childhood, handbagged and hatted-
    and-gloved,
who tutted and tidied our hair and our collars and conscience,
who saw that our manners were laced up and laundered and
    combed,
who reproved any wilfulness, offered us wonders
that widened and gloried our world –
who laughed and relaxed with their books, with their teacups
    and tennis,
with song, or with sequins of wit from their side-slipping
    mouths –
it seemed that they changed as we grew.

For a while we were equals. Our eyes shared experience
woman to woman. Our talking caught fire and we spoke
of the comfort and pain and the depth of the blood, reassured.
But they went on ahead – became fragile, forgetful,
rehearsed for that final departure.
So we're down to our very last aunt.

Kin

Bone of bone.
Long-gone grandmother's
turn of phrase
zips
between cousins.
Quirk of mouth,
sidewise crack of wit.
The kettle steams.
Eye-bright, eye-dim.
His stance. Her gaze.
'Hair like your own!
Those fingers, see!'
And a twist of sound –
faint silver tune
on a son's lips –
my father's, his before him,
riding home.

The Nightingale

for a poet hard of hearing

In that old tale
gleaned from soft and speckled pages
smuggled under sheets, read by torchlight,
an emperor had a nightingale.
Created by a genius,
it clacked and whirred,
and preened its jewelled wings
in metal imitation of the bird.
My childhood mind
avoided the didactics of the tale,
but relished detail of the cog-wheeled filigree,
the feather-fine precision, neat and frail.
My inward ear delighted in the sound;
the tiny clicks and stutters and the thin
mechanic hesitation held me bound.
Never mind the moral. It's
the image that applies.
Your deaf voice holds the echoes of that sound.
No matter. From your pages rise
your true tones, music of the living nightingale.

Honeyeaters

So neat the honeyeater flips, nips,
nip and tuck on the bowing branch,
the branching bough,
dips its beak to nip and sip
from rose-jelly colour hair-roller pin curls of grevillea
drawing its strength from their strong sweet,
like sailors trapezing,
like acrobats dangling, comically skilful,
but focussed and savage,
fierce and neat as a nurse unpicking sutures.

Agapanthus

'here is the church
here is the steeple,
open the doors,
and there are the people'
        child's finger game

Slender-columned minarets.
Copper-blue glow of ancient mosques.
Matte green in the noon heat,
beaded with crystal at dawn.
Tall, silent, serene.
Peeling like paperbark as the buds swell,
stretch, split open to reveal
clusters of turbaned heads quiet within.
Reverent blue, gentle white,
silent in worship, still in prayer.
Summer's muezzin, the bee,
calls agapanthus to sing –
opening, burgeoning now,
paeans of azure and carols of white.
Joy is its season and courage its name.
A flower, a church, or a mosque are the same.

The Outback

Out there the stars swarm like bees,
hang humming with light
just beyond fingertip reach.
The skies are dark in the way that plums glow
blackly violet and juicy with light among leaves.

Out there the dawn's a red line
scored with a poker, scorching the world's rim,
straight as a margin far beyond aeons of grasses.
Only the weary-faced moon stands in the sky
clouded over with parakeets and galahs meeting the day.

At Bonny Hills

The colour of the sea is tears on silk.

The coral-trees and native figs lean landward,
roped to the soil with roots as taut as hawsers.
Down the cliff-face hang she-oak, bitou bush, lantana,
fringed at the top with renegades from town –
shepherd's purse and daisy, thistledown and dock.
Two stick-men sleek as seals and pinhead-size
bob blackly in the curves of surf. Waves roll over rocks
chopped square and brown as chocolate,
then come feathering over the sand as sweet
as Sunday handkerchiefs.
When the sun skims back the haze, the colours shift –
cloud-shadows roam the paddocks of green water,
grazing on pastures for the soul.
Inland there are fires, past summers sending messages.
Framed in fiery bottlebrush the ocean claws the land
flinging and flinging its white-knuckled fists at the shore.
amid the grass discarded seashells lie,
clenching tight their whorls of silence.

The cast-iron banksias clash their metal leaves.

Norfolk Island Pine

Mast and spars of a tall ship,
the pine looms behind our trees,
anchored in dream waters just beyond our garden.
Precise as a clipper's its crossbars spread
wide at the base, narrowing to the crow's nest
and tipped with pine-cone mooring lights.
On a day of wild gusts, half hidden by the wind
are the cries of old sailors
and the fifes and the drums of departure.

Grandmother Lily's Babies

When she was very old and tended by her daughter
she'd be found o' nights beside her tumbled bed,
standing hunched and gentle where a phantom cradle held
her long-dead babies. There were three she buried,
little white-faced mewling creatures silenced soon
by unknown ills fly-borne in dusty summers, chilled to wax
   by cold.

When I, lost in her unfamiliar house and dreaming,
wandered to her bedroom late at night,
what did she think, to see a white-clad child bewildered
hesitating at her door? Oh, Lillian! When you wrapped
your lean arms tight around me, was it me you held
so fiercely in the dark, or did you think that they'd come back
   again?

November Dawn

Bushfire haze stretched like a tarp
tree-height, straight over the world,
exactly the cloud grey of that scrap you'll remember
from childhood, the delicate Japanese silk.

The moon shone weak as a torch bulb
through a dusty mosquito net of haze.
Only the eastern edge of the cloud glowed crimson,
drenching the pavers in puddles of fire.
The little frog in the jasmine uttered his lonely clonk.
The Labrador paused to sift the air's strangeness
then, vast and amiable as a bear, creaked from her
basket and cantered down the veranda.

You'd think ruby droplets of light
should scatter around her.

Child and Bushfire, 1942

This is a voice in my blood,
The Black and Tans were terrible men in Ireland years ago,
rolling over the countryside and bringing death,
choking our green hope.
But now is the year half Australia is blowing away to sea,
This is my seventh year, and the sun hangs green
showing its bilious face amid curtains of black, of tan.
Smoke from the fires and the billowing inland dust.
Our forefathers were giants, their women heroic,
but their horse-drawn harrows, their cross-cut saws,
the myriad pattering cloven feet
of the foolish mad-eyed innocent sheep,
have brought the land undone. They laboured at clearing,
gave the blood of their hands and the sweat of their backs
in shaping the rolling plains of wheat.
Now after years of drought, bushfires
have roused the battalions of dust. For weeks
like a blinded eye the sun hangs livid,
blinks mauve or blue or lime, weeps pallid tears of light
through the sky's blanket of topsoil and smoke,
its ravaging black and tan.

Last Day of Winter

The morning went in tending the rose bed.
Winks of colour budding here and there
prompting action – rose food, water,
tucking the rugs of mulch round their toes.

Later we sat cradling our mugs
and watching jets' drawn threadwork in the sky;
long stitches, over blue and under clouds,
the mare's-tail cloud that hints of rain.

The evening fire outglowed the rose and apricot
of winter's final sunset in the trees.
I tossed on marjoram and rosemary,
propitiating all the smaller gods, and thought of you.

Tomorrow will be spring. The frosts are done.
Stars bloom whitely in our southern sky.
Sisters, mothers, love, and death,
stir among the embers, whisper me to sleep.

Saying Goodbye

Hard enough when it's people,
hardest with old dogs whose peat-pool eyes
hold loving farewell in their deep.
But how to say a last goodbye to leaves,
to sand airbrushed in circles
by the swinging kiss of grass,
and how, oh how, to skies?

Green Sky

Over the farmhouse roof a tall sky stands,
as clean and cool as pistachio cream;
and sweet as a christening a thread of moon
snapped from a crystal filament
and tossed there, trembles on the green.
Just for a moment everything is still.
The sun is far below the mountains, yet
like a last message lit with peach and gold
a jet trail's silent progress as the plane
neatly rules a line to end the day.

Visiting the Specialists

You're on a plateau now, they said, with medication
nicely balanced against side effects. We'll get
the dosage down of course, but slowly, testing all the while.
Because that stuff's not good for you although
it's doing good. You're feeling well?
I'm feeling great. It's not so good to know
that what has made my limbs as limber as a ten-year-old
and dampens down the dizziness and feverish fatigue
is also working evil in the tunnels of my marrow-bones,
is lurking in my nerve ends and shorting out my brain,
so what should be a tableland with views across the valleys
feels far more like a sword edge and God help me should I slip.

Plover

Plover's gait is run-and-stop-run-and-stop.
Stilted run, wary stop.
Tread close accidentally and see
the plover's jewel in the grass,
such frail and freckled treasure.
Speckled eggs within a simple nest,
the merest indentation in the sand
among the pebbles and the threads of root.
Love makes the plover limp away
drag-winged and seeming-wounded,
luring the eye from her frail-shelled delicate hope.
Hear in the night the clamorous plover's cry –
imagine a didgeridoo, but shrill –
throbbing, insistently throbbing its minor alarm,
stridently screeching and jaggedly scraping the dark.
We stir in our sleep, for a moment
aware of your call then turning and drifting away.
What is your fright, bird, is it dogs, is it dreams,
is it fear for a child come to harm?
That shallowest scoop in the sand holds treasure,
holds for the lapwing old magic and power,
It is Love sends the plover to shriek and to rail at the night.

Beethoven's Child

That rumour of Beethoven's child enthrals me,
pacing the plastic rattle of eucalyptus leaves
and the crackle of gum nuts underfoot,
where a blue sky scarred by crows
is filled with his music.
Gazing at spindrift clouds swift as old movies,
a scherzo of breeze in the feathers and beads of the wattle.
Or, parked with hot pies on a headland of bitou bush,
there's a runnelling windscreen, the radio playing his music,
squalls curtaining half the horizon
and the white-haired sea thrashing the sand.
And when frosts of stars powder the night sky
sonata and fugue flutter with flames in the grate.
Symphonies spin with the falling of leaves,
the ruby and wine that tumble from brick-hugging vines.
And in all weathers the rumour of Beethoven's child
continues to play counterpoint to his music.

Two Weddings...Tuncurry and Kosovo

In a bombshell blast of tulle the bride
caught by cameras, poses on the driveway –
lacy grenade, her bouquet's tossed,
guests swirl and break like fighters scattering –
with gunshot cracks her veil snaps in the wind.

In Kosovo the bridegroom's name is Death;
oh clasp the hands of children blown apart,
deck for this different wedding scarlet, white,
the soil where other guests have passed.
See, there are flowers here – bouquets of red.

The wind that tugs the bride's veil here
has other work to do in Kosovo.

Breath Music

flautist Jane Rutter speaking on ABC's *Sunday Afternoon*, 1999

Instruments of the breath –
flutes and bamboo pipes, like singing –
come from closest to the heart,
nearest the spirit, speak directly to the soul.
So too your music. So, in little,
is my verse, could I but read to you.

Courage

Today a long-neck tortoise came
on fleshless lizard legs,
like the old men at the nursing-home
so slow he moved it hurt me.
He'd that bared-mummy skin and uncut nails;
the ragged tangle of his bird-pecked shell
had just the dangle of the careless dressing-gowns
my dad and all those others had about them.
He poked his head and goggled at the water tin,
mistrusting it as dad felt wary of the nurses:
they want what they can get. Untrue –
but he'd been thrown and rolled-on by the years
as any rogue horse will, his farmer's eyesight
blackened, all his world shrunk down
to a dim circle in a strange country.
Still he pushed on in spirit through this wasteland.
In such a way, the tortoise crept across our lawn.

Near Black Bob's Creek, Southern Highlands, NSW

Car radio rippled us over the hills
through heartbreak green of willow on old boughs
and clouds like underbellies of a mammoth herd.
Over a velvet hill as smooth as a stage set
a corps de ballet of plum trees fluffed their tutus,
linked arms and trippingly advanced
in caracoling line toward the road.
Near here we saw the signboard – Black Bob's Creek

Was ebony-browed and bearded Bob a brawler once,
in some shin-splintering skin-slitting shindy here,
among a shamble of black-tempered Irishmen?

Was Bob, like old 'Banana' up in Queensland,
a working bullock of a famous team,
heaved them once to safety in a fabled flood time,
dropped in his patient traces when his life was done?

Was he a shadow from a hounded tribe,
shuffling for the white man's baccy and flour,
wordless to explain his kinship with the earth
but hiving an old wisdom in his bones,
storing it against a day to come?

And when the government men came through
surveying, labelling, did some remembering local say,
Ar well, there was an old bloke once lived up and down the river,
blackfella…always said this was his country.
O'course, we laughed, but still…his eyes said something…
ar we call it Black Bob's Creek.

Or were we too romantic? Did it mean
that in the muddy caverns of the creek
those dark-as-midnight yabbies, craw-bobs,
clashed and fumbled with their robot claws
and dodged the farm boys with their baited string?

Rainbow Bee-eaters

Two rainbow birds came to our tree.
Crisp as lemon leaves the folded wing,
close to the crackled bark they'd cling,
from ringed and delicate throats
their talk would click and creak –
we thought their voices crickets. There they sat
turning their wary heads from side to side
alert as sentries pausing for a chat,
then in turn went flashing bright,
dancing in circles overhead;
wings as sharp as the Norfolk pine
of opal-shimmering taffeta light
they clipped the air in wing-snip flight.

Was there a nest? It secret lay,
but pride of chirrup, wand of wing,
such magic-circling in the air
spoke clear to parents such as we
and gave the truth away.

All parents know their witchcraft well.
To ward the nest from harm
thrice-woven circles of the air,
that ancient frail protection-plea,
that shield of tears and candle flame,
that fragile web of hope and prayer.

We share this with them and we know
all magic spells are bluff. As we,
the birds know witchcraft's shadow stuff.
Oh heaven forfend
the rainbow-bird found dead upon the road
was one of that brave pair!
Its shot-silk wing was fading even then.
its lacy plume became a dart
that struck into the finder's heart.
Oh heed my song –
we cannot hold them, rainbow-birds or children,
not for long.

Song Strata

In thin black scratches, cockies' screeches scrape the sky
and, threaded through, exasperated laughter
as the kookaburra notes absurdity.
Lower down the wooden clack and rattle of the friar birds,
the curves and loops of sound that swoop from swifts,
and shivering below,
the silvery calls of magpies dropping down and down,
the cricket-crake of rainbow birds,
the honeyeater's carnival oy-oy.
At tea tree level chirping wrens,
a flitter of chittering finches,
the wattlebird's bamboo clatter,
curls of koel calls.
Swamp pheasant drops
a booming hoot from velvet throat
and then a tumbling string of bead-like notes.
At garden height
a golden shimmer of insect voices, crickets
backed by curtains of cicada noise,
the bass and homely comfort of the frogs.
Swallows swing and chatter.
Then a rondelay of solo chorus as the sun goes down.

Peeling Peaches

Now do I mourn my mother,
now that the roses are in bloom
and summer lizards skip across the terracotta
immaculate in pattern, pert and trim.
Oh now I mourn her
as fruit-preserving time begins
and peaches perfumed, fleshed
so greenly-succulently-white,
greet summer with their sueded rosy cheeks.
Oh now I mourn:
for peaches, penny-lizards, roses were her loves;
and I recall
her fingers smooth as ivory
wielding the black knife as velvet peelings fell away
in the summer-scented kitchen.
She winked in wry amusement telling how
the tiny skink came bicycling toward her,
propped and reared and spat defiance.

Her eyes in one flash laughed, lamented,
scorned her own emotion, praised
the matchstick creature's valour,
knew its fate.
Now when the tang of peaches stings
like her sharp wit,
when penny-lizards pedal on the path,
their tiny pride an echo of her own,
that frailty defiant;
now when the silk of the rose
crumples and blows on the wind;
Oh now I mourn her,
now, in the season of peaches.

Driving North

The road unrolls beneath us like a spool of tape,
black ribbon notched with white
winding and unwinding towards our wheels.
Driving north through clouds and rainbows,
driving north with the radio on,
we go from what we are to what we will become.
A milky sun dodges the boxing-glove clouds,
floodwaters sheet the world on either side,
flamenco music chokes the air with bitter honey,
and we are driving north to her ninetieth birthday.
Coolongalook – a flock of egrets
flings up like a flapped cloth,
like a sheet cracked in the wind,
settles again on limbs of wading trees.
Near Lansdowne pub choppy waves cut the road,
hot-gospelling sun shafts preach to flooded paddocks,
the farms marooned, the sodden hay.
The threads of music change to Arabic guitar.

Wading farm-wives walk their milkers home.
Does she recall her mornings and the milking,
the baby cradled in a fruit box and the scrubbed-raw children?
Grafton to Casino – spindle-shanked the dreary bush slips by
and pine plantations dark with European shadows.
Vivaldi threads and reels the long road in,
pulls hills towards us, leaves the floods behind.
Through dreams and destinies we go
to reach our journey's ending.
Oh who will come and in what weather,
to what tunes and what imaginings
drive towards the last stop on *our* road?
The radio, the roads, the waters say
we're driving north to what we will become.

Pelican

Old
pelican
riding the sky,
gallant old frigate
full-sail, tilt-winged,
keel-bellied as a seaplane,
cannily snatching the updraught,
gliding away.
Was that you or your brother
grumpily hunched on the jetty,
stumpily clumping and lurching about
waddle-legged,
with your wobbling wattled old man's throat
agape and agawk at the fisherman's loot?
Both had a similar
humorist's
eye.

After Winter Rain

The cherry tree's become a chandelier.
Black parasol ribs curve down,
bedecked with beads of crystal,
and in the pale dawn's rise
these flare and gleam.

Jacaranda

Warmer than blue,
as loving is warmer, and giving,
brimful of blessing,
your blossom
spills over us now.
Bountiful giver of beauty,
beautiful giver of shade,
jacaranda,
breathe your sweet word.

King Parrots

Over the half-dark grass two king parrots.
Enough light to see they were clad
in the hail-heavy green of a storm and the red of a sunrise.
Holding our breath – oh will you stay –
as they strolled sleepily along branches
scraping their beaks, curving their heads to preen,
chirruping soft conversation,
around them the swift darts of swallow and honeyeater
and once the soft flit of a bat.
Thinking of you faraway and last summer,
how you swooped home and our breath stopped
– oh will you stay –
while morning heightened their colour,
brought out the blue and the markings.
Mission completed. Away.
And that was you, too, last summer.
Now there are
sounds of wet-weather summer birds,
the swamp pheasant, whipbird,
the gamelan *tok* of a bamboo throat
in the wet luminous morning.

Not the TV News

Skies do my weather forecast –
clouds mass and boom, threaten,
disperse, form mackerel or mares' tails,
melt into hot blue;
ahead of rain birds speed low,
ants scurry to bring in stores,
shore up entries,
scribble their thin black lines along the path,
marking the weather map's highs and lows.
Trees broadcast the news –
rumour of wind, disaster of broken branch,
bombardment and terror of crashing trunk,
beetle and nestling in refugee mode,
flame in the forest,
obituary in the mouldering leaves,
scandal and pseudo-shock in the twining of boughs.
Butterflies flaunt, provide the celebrity shots,
while a bug or a cricket is bound to be there
for that sugary item that winds up the news.

Epitaph for a Very Small Dog

Leaves rattle along the path.
Cherry trees bare umbrella ribs.
Dawn dew chills like frost. The clouds
stagger and lurch across the sky.
The smallest dog, magpies' Boudicca,
the mop-headed pesky survivor,
that raggedy yapper who twirled
pirouettes on the pathway, led all
charges, dominated the household,
my little old rag-mop friend, bird-boned,
light as a kitten, who'd dance a greeting,
speak wise or merry with her liquid eyes
to hold my heart from old despair,
lies now beneath roses and stone,
under the scarlet and gold of cherry leaves.
Sadness in autumn.
   Despite my tears
she dances on thimble-sized feet,
shakes her pencil-stub tail,
follows wherever I go, and at night
still curls on my pillow,
snug as two sleepy handfuls of silk.

Bad Weather

I like horses and roses and days
when the heart doesn't ache,
violets and pigeons and times
when the knife in the bone holds still,
walking and sunrise and words
that say what I feel;
but not shipwreck mornings like this,
cold air from the hills and rain from the sea,
when the wind blows crankiness into your skin
and boredom drips damply under the collar.
They're gritty, irascible, aimless days
when the castaway crotchety soul washes up
on do-nothing island. Can't write!
Any bread you may toss on these waters
goes soggy and sinks.

Two Roses

A tribute to two strong old women who gave me rose cuttings – and good plain talk when it was needed!

You notice yourself growing older, said Jean,
snug among hand-painted china in twinset and tweed,
specklessly neat in retirement from classrooms and proud
of the Sunday school's farewell gift; a widow, a gran,
my kindliest mentor, all lacy and lavendered
prisms and prunes. *But it's nothing till seventy comes*
she rapped at me sharp as a shot, grim as a grave,
prim as a pin. *Then you look down the throat
of a black-hearted gun.*

Gwen was the last of a silvertail dynasty, perky and petulant,
ruled like a matriarch, couldn't quite shake
her autocracy off when she dealt with the neighbours,
pottered and gardened and held to her big-house airs.
It's a very old rose, a survivor, she said, *one of the gardeners told
me its name, long ago*…and her eyes held faraway images,
glimpses we gathered of grandeur and sea trips,
the wool clip that paid for the manicured acres,
though paying's too vulgar a term.

For a boon, when the time comes and the gun barrel swings
my way, could you add to the scales that they both
godmothered my ageing, the way good fairies do at a birth?
Two tough old women – Jean with her calm and her strength
and her plain pink rose, Gwen who when age was importunate
made hers an aristocrat's end, ramming a tree with the Jag.
God grant me their gaunt grained grip – theirs, and that of
the roses they gave me, survivors, outriders of death,
in their honest pink gingham and pearls upon apricot silk.

Autumn Afternoon

Autumn holds no drowsiness –
there's a crispness to its amber-rose
tells us the end of things,
the end of things and their beginning.

Light through leaves.
The sky's chill blue.
The sun burns through my sleeve
yet has a thread-thin edge
as sharp as racing cloud.

Hold this moment –
the child's voice, his curled fingers,
the ruby leaf.
the end of things and their beginning.

www.ingramcontent.com/pod-product-compliance
Lightning Source LLC
Chambersburg PA
CBHW070102120526
44589CB00033B/1549